G000109609

Oh, No Dear!

Advice to Girls a Century Ago

Oh, No Dear!

Advice to Girls a Century Ago

Selected and compiled by
ROY HINDLE

DAVID & CHARLES
Newton Abbot London North Pomfret (Vt)

For my friends
Fred and Sheila Snowden—
they will know why

British Library Cataloguing in Publication Data

Oh, no dear!: advice to girls a century ago.
1. Adolescent girls—Conduct of life
2. Counseling—Great Britain
I. Hindle, Roy
362.7'042 HQ798

ISBN 0-7153-8330-2

Typeset by ABM Typographics Limited, Hull
and printed in Great Britain
by Butler & Tanner, Frome
for David & Charles (Publishers) Limited
Brunel House Newton Abbot Devon

Published in the United States of America
by David & Charles Inc
North Pomfret Vermont 05053 USA

PREFACE

The Girl's Own Paper was first published, 'Price One Penny', on 3 January 1880, in a world remarkably different from our own.

In 1880 Queen Victoria was in the forty-third year of her reign and Gladstone became her Prime Minister for the second time. Although the monarch was a woman, females in general were regarded as second-class citizens. Single women had little freedom to do as they chose; for married women there were fewer social restrictions but financial freedom remained severely curtailed, even if the money had originally been their own.

The waltz was the dance of the day. Johann Strauss' latest was 'Roses from the South', following the thirteen-year-old 'Blue Danube'; the 'Voices of Spring' were not to be heard for another two years. Lawn tennis, at first called Sphairistike, was only six years old, but girls were already taking it up, albeit in hats, gloves and full-length dresses.

Though there were 18,000 miles of railways in Britain, corridor trains did not exist and the Pullman dining car had only just arrived. There were bicycles, both bone-shakers and penny-farthings, all 'quite unsuited for the use of girls', but no pneumatic tyres and no internal combustion engines, so most road transport depended upon the horse, either ridden or driven. The first automobile was thirteen years away.

Cooking was mostly with solid fuel, though gas had been gaining in popularity over the last ten years; cooking utensils were mostly iron or earthenware, aluminium was a scarce metal and stainless steel another thirty years away. Few houses had proper indoor sanitation and the chamber pot was a household essential. Artificial lighting was by gas, paraffin lamps or candles, but the gas-mantle which so greatly increased and steadied the light of the gas burner was six years off. Cholera still presented a menace but was being brought under control; the last major outbreak in London occurred in 1866, when more than 5,000 died.

Income tax, regarded at this date as nothing more than a temporary measure, was 5d. in the £1 (2.08 per cent). There was no old-age pension nor unemployment benefit.

Poverty had sharp teeth and, with parish relief difficult to obtain, the inevitable result was large numbers of tramps and beggars.

In 1880 the President of the United States was Rutherford Birchard Hayes, 'a third rate nonentity, whose only recommendation is that he was obnoxious to no one'. The President's wife was an ardent teetotaller, so at White House receptions 'the water flowed like wine'. The same year saw the beginning of street-lighting in New York, a city which had not yet acquired either its characteristic skyscrapers or the Statue of Liberty. There were nine years to wait for the Eiffel Tower — and the roll-film on which to photograph it. Winston Churchill and Marconi were both six years old, Lenin was ten, Trotsky three and Stalin a year-old baby.

Although a number of periodicals of various types had already been issued, all of those intended for children prior to *The Boy's Own Paper,* which was first published in 1879, were intensely moral and aimed first and foremost at improving the minds and souls of the young readers. *The Boy's Own Paper*, though retaining a firm religious base, was freer in its outlook and much more entertaining. *The Girl's Own Paper* was from the same publishers, with the same broader view and range, and was the first-ever paper intended solely for girls. It seems to have been aimed principally at the older schoolgirl and the younger adult woman in fairly well-to-do circumstances. There are many references to girls aged thirteen and above who were expected to stay at school until they were eighteen, whilst the annual volumes were offered in variously coloured bindings including white 'for wedding presents'. The readership, however, was evidently wider and included both much older women and servants, though in the case of the latter the paper was probably handed down from 'above stairs'; even one penny a week was a consideration to a girl earning only £10 or less a year.

Typewriters (the word originally referred to the operator, not the machine) had been available for only seven years, so great importance was still attached to a high standard of handwriting, both in commerce and in private life, and the Editor of *The Girl's Own Paper* hammered this point home in his replies to correspondents. Perhaps the emphasis on beautiful and legible writing as a vital ingredient in character formation, and the constant copy-book practice thought necessary, accounts for the editorial discouragement of more imaginative writing such as poetry.

'This magazine', the prospectus promised, 'will aim at being to the girls a Counsellor, Playmate, Guardian, Instructor, Companion, and Friend. It will help to train them in moral and domestic virtues, preparing them for the responsibilities of womanhood, and for a heavenly home.' Within a few months the Editor claimed to be receiving nearly a thousand letters a week, of which on average about seventy were selected for 'Answers to Correspondents'. The questions were not published, and it is sometimes very difficult (or downright impossible) to deduce what they were. If anyone can explain the answer to SCOTT, I shall be very glad to know.

From some 10,000 replies published between 1880 and 1882 I have chosen nearly five hundred. I hope that the selection of answers reprinted in this book will, in addition to showing that much has changed in the course of a century, prove a source of interest, amusement and occasional amazement to today's readers. All the replies are genuine — even the one advising 'Wash with soap and water, and then whitewash all over.'

R.H.

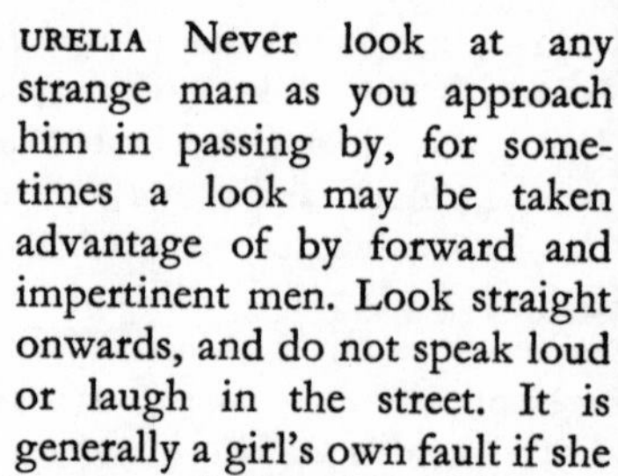

AURELIA Never look at any strange man as you approach him in passing by, for sometimes a look may be taken advantage of by forward and impertinent men. Look straight onwards, and do not speak loud or laugh in the street. It is generally a girl's own fault if she be spoken to, and, as such, is a disgrace to her, of which she should be ashamed to speak. But we must hope and believe that the liberties thus taken were owing to no light manner, nor indiscreet conduct in your case.

SARAH We fear there is no way of curing the unpleasant creaking noise, which is caused by the glue mixed with the dye. Use any of the varnishes sold for polishing boots and shoes to your hat, or a wash of black sealing-wax dissolved in alcohol.

MAGGIE Much of the bodily strength goes to the hair, and if a child be delicate it is advisable to shorten it to a certain extent.

ROWENA We think that a girl of seventeen or eighteen is too young to wear a cap in the evening. No pattern would be required if you wished to make one. You need only to bend a piece of ribbon-wire round your head, and cover it with a loose crown of velvet or other material, and then tack on an edging of lace as deep as may be becoming.

KIT Perhaps rubbing with flour would clean your white rabbits that made an eccentric excursion up a chimney.

SHAMROCK Bicycles are quite unsuited for the use of girls. You might employ a tricycle in the country, or in the appointed place in South Kensington, where a ladies' club has, we believe, been formed.

MISS GREENHORN Do not meddle with your arms at all; wear long mittens or gloves, or else sleeves long enough to hide them. Black slippers may be worn with crimson stockings and mittens. Black gloves may still be worn in the evening, but light colours are more usual.

SOPHIA Sealskin caps or turbans will be much used by young girls this winter. They are quite inexpensive, and have a large spreading looped bow of coloured ribbon over the top of the crown.

BOTHER OF A GIRL We do not remember having seen a cheap edition of the book you name. Why not use a little vaseline?

CLAITHA The colour of pearls may be improved and preserved by keeping a bit of the root of an ash tree in the box where they are kept.

LILLIE MORE We feel very much the enormous responsibility you have placed upon us in asking us to advise you on entering the profession to which you refer. But we dare not do other than counsel you to abandon all ideas of thus engaging yourself. Believe us you are not alone in your particular aspirations. Most girls above the ordinary abilities have the same unhealthy craving at some particular period of their life, but when they grow older and see how incongruous is that position to a good honest girl's they are filled with a life-long thankfulness that they did not join the profession. In addition to great abilities, unusual physical strength, and personal attractions, a Christian girl or woman would need the steadfastness of a more than Job or St. Paul to come out unscathed from the fiery ordeal. We happen to know many things of the life and character of the lady you mention which would lead you to either despise or pity her very much.

LADY CLARICE We quote, for the benefit of our hysterical correspondent, from a first-class medical work recently published: 'If a girl wishes to have an hysterical fit, by all means let her have it. Conduct her to an empty room, place her on the floor, and let her have a fit quietly by herself.'

NELLIE The 'poke' bonnets of black straw are quite as much worn as ever only they are bent rather flatter, and wider in front. If yours be lined with black velvet, it would not need new lining for the winter. If however, you wish for a change from the red bows and black lining, try some old-gold coloured ribbon instead, and a small black feather. Line the bonnet also with old-gold satin. Three yards and a half of the ribbon should make the new bonnet and the strings, and three-quarters of a yard of old-gold satin cut on the bias, and divided into three pieces, will make the fashionable gathered lining. This will change the appearance of the bonnet completely, at an expense of 5s. [25p] carefully laid out.

CHERRY RIPE You may cleanse steel by rubbing on it a mixture composed of an ounce of camphor and a pound of hog's lard, mixed with as much blacklead as will give the mixture an iron colour. Leave this on the steel for two days, and rub off with a linen cloth. It may also be used during the summer to preserve steel from rust when unused.

SPES We should think that having passed both the senior and the junior Cambridge, you ought to obtain at least £40 per annum, but there can be no rule as to salaries.

ANNE We hope that your question on the supposed privileges of ladies during leap year was only put to us in fun. No girl, having any self-respect, would do such a thing.

UNDINE What you call 'high tea' does take the place of a late dinner; and as the dinner hour varies according to the convenience or fancy of the mistress of the house, so may 'high tea'. With the exception of joints of meat, soup, and vegetables, most viands may be used for it. Cold pies and tarts, cold chickens, ham, brawn, fish, eggs in all forms, omelettes, potted meats, scalloped oysters, stewed mushrooms, kidneys, fruit, cheesecakes, and tartlets; puddings and hot cakes of all kinds are suitable for it. But tea, coffee, and chocolate are substituted for wine and beer.

F.E.T.R. We should strongly advise you not to work up for the examination, as it would most probably ruin what little health you have.

IRENE F. The siege of Saragossa took place in 1809. The name of Augustina Zaragoza, the 'Maid of Saragossa', has been especially preserved as that of the bravest among the women of the city, who all worked, and exposed themselves with their respective fathers, brothers, and husbands.

ANNIE AUDREY Feed the white mice on corn, canary seed, bread etc, but never give them cheese. Hay does very well for a bed, and so does white cotton wool; black cotton wool kills them, as we have learned from experience.

POOR FIFTEEN For the growing out of the shoulder-blades it will be necessary to use a back-board; and if necessary a face-board too.

H.A.M. Take this as a safe guide for your actions: never go where you would be indisposed, on account of the unsuitableness of the place, to offer up a prayer to God.

GRATEFUL Will you send us some of the flies? In the meantime, we should suggest covering the wire with gauze.

MOONBEAM Take off your mittens when playing the violin or piano. Write 'Violoncello'. Ladies sometimes play it now.

FAD As you do not like to use the powders sold to kill cockroaches you must get a tame hedgehog.

LORELEI It is by no means fit for a young lady or any lady, to ride alone in the country.

A YOUNG HORSEWOMAN is referred to the answer given to 'Lorelei'. She ought to consult her mother or guardian as to the propriety of riding after hounds under the guardianship of a gentleman. Much depends on who he is, and, if suitable, whether he never leaves her side.

W.G.B. We are much obliged to you for your kind note and the lines on 'Friendship'. We are sorry to hear that you are rather fond of putting your thoughts into rhyme, because we think it a great waste of time, and unless you had been properly taught to write in rhyme, you should not attempt it. We regret we cannot print your 'poem' as a warning to others, but we hope from this time forth you will devote yourself to more useful things.

LADY EDYTHE The word 'requiem' is pronounced as if spelt 'reequiem'. Try syringing the ears.

MARGUERITE S. We have been much pleased with the excellent washing and wearing qualities of workhouse sheeting, used for curtains; and think you would like it.

Make the window and fireplace curtains of the same, and scald the crewels you employ.

EDEN BAPTIST We are pleased to hear that you value the cold bath as it should be valued. Your handwriting is peculiar, but not unpleasantly so. Be careful with your f's. They are very awkward looking.

HILDA W. S. (1) No one should have less than eight hours of sleep in the twenty-four. (2) Try laying a handkerchief across the forehead when you go to bed dipped in Eau sedative and water.

LADY CHEVELEY is thanked for her kind praise of this paper. Long shreds of letter paper cut as narrow as the blade of a penknife will prove a fair substitute for feathers to stuff a cushion.

E.K. How dare you write to us about the enamel paint? Write to your own magazine, *The Boy's Own Paper*. We delight in affording pleasure and benefit to the fair sex only.

BENMORE Pronounce Thucydides as if written 'Thu-cid-did-ees'; and Euripides as 'You-rip-e-dees'. Your writing and manners appear to have been much neglected.

DAPHNE Wear cashmere shoes and boots.

NESTA The reason for knitting the wool is to cause it to wave like moss after a wetting and baking. It is done in plain knitting on steel needles. Before writing again to us please try the instructions given, you will then see the effect. Fill the box with sand if you choose.

EXCELSIOR Ferns in a glass case need water and care like any other plants. Wear muslin frills round your neck.

PEPITA If the mourning be for one of the heads of the house, the servants should have two dresses each, a print, and a coburg.

WOODBINE Oatmeal stirabout is very wholesome, though to take it more than once a day might be too heating.

SWEET FIFTEEN (1) To preserve black stockings from turning brown when washed, dip them first into a mixture of half a teacupful of spirits of turpentine to one quart of water. (2) Wash the meat with a weak solution of Condy's Fluid, cut out equivocal looking parts, and cover it to keep the flies away.

TIGER LILY You do not mention your age, so we cannot answer your inquiry 'Am I too old for your competitions?'

KAFFOOSELEM Please go to the nearest greenhouse and market garden, and obtain the answers to the string of questions with which you have favoured us.

MAY When you meet any one a second time, the recognition should be more in a slight smile than a bow; the inclination of the head should be scarcely observable.

VIOLET SILVER asks for 'a receipt for red hands'. We have none to acknowledge. If she requires a recipe for them we advise her to wear no gloves, and expose them successively to sun and frost.

ANDROMEDA The new postage stamps as now printed are very much cheaper than the old ones, and they have the advantage of a colour that is not of a poisonous nature.

MOLLY 'Gooseberry fool' is a corruption of 'gooseberry foul', from *foulé*, a French word meaning mashed or pressed. Cut the nails in a rounded or oval shape.

VALERIA If not allowed to heat your room by any kind of stove, and you have no chimney or fireplace, we recommend you to supply yourself with a large tin or stone jar to be replenished from time to time with hot water.

WHITE ROSE AND NYMPH We think £25 would be a sufficient allowance for you to dress upon. Seventeen is very young to leave school.

IRISH GIRL Your mother should be consulted in reference to the introduction you wish to make. If she approve your course is clear, but you must confide all you know to her respecting your acquaintance before you act upon any permission you may obtain.

RUBY Black velvet is most ladylike, but some figures are improved by variety of trimming.

SANDY CAT Fill every aperture, and cover the shelves of the larder with table salt. Otherwise you may catch them by means of a few cabbage leaves rubbed over with dripping or unsalted butter. In a few hours they will be covered with slugs.

LITTLE NIPPER asks 'Can you tell me the name of any poem where the conceit of men is *particually* named?' No, we cannot, but we know a paper in which is portrayed the conceit of girls — and that is the far-famed *Girl's Own Paper.*

OUR MARY You say that your 'canpain' wishes to ask 'if is too young to comane singing; she can't go hight, she would like to be a teacher of a sing school and a police'. If unable to write, spell, and express herself better than you do at fourteen, we doubt her ever being competent to act as a teacher of anything.

SPEEDWELL Up to the present time [May 1880] the Houses of Parliament at Westminster have cost about £3,000,000. They cover about nine acres of land. The works were commenced in 1837 by an embankment 886 feet in length; the building itself was begun in 1840. The whole edifice stands on a bed of concrete twelve feet thick; to the east it has a front of 1,000 feet. It contains 1,100 apartments, 100 staircases, and about two miles of passages or corridors. The Victoria Tower, through which the Queen passes to open Parliament, is 336 feet in height. The architect was Sir Charles Barry (born 1795, died 1860).

CRYSTAL Neuralgic pains have many causes, tight boots being sometimes one.

ANTIGONE If the gentleman be a relative, a present on his marriage is usual and right. Pour on boiling water and rub well with hearthstone.

MRS TYLER Your request that we should recommend you the use of some drug to stop the growth of your daughter, and even, as you express it, to 'shorten her', is a disgrace to you. Thank God, on the contrary, that He has given you a fine child who grows well, and seems to thrive in spite of your very unnatural wishes to stunt her growth. It could not be done; and any attempt to do it would destroy her health.

MARY ELIZABETH You did quite right to try the sulphur ointment, and you may still use it for about a fortnight; if the cat's hair does not show signs of returning naturally then, use a dressing of mild ammonia liniment once a day. Any chemist can prepare this for you, but you had better tell him the purpose for which you want to use it. It may be improved by the addition of a little tincture of Spanish flies.

POMMES DE TERRE We believe that the author respecting whom you inquire is still living; but we have no desire to 'shed some light on his ancestors', to which proceeding we entertain *grave* objections.

ADELAIDE Do not waste your time on writing poetry, read some good history or poetry by some of the great masters of the art, instead; by doing so you will cultivate a much more healthy state of mind.

CALABASH There is no real 'above and beneath' the earth, but some of the celestial bodies are, of course, in the heavens of the antipodes, if you like to call the latter portion of the globe 'beneath' you. The laws of gravitation, holding you closely to the ground on which you stand, are so ordered as to allow of you feeling no inconvenience from the rotary movement of the earth.

BLACKBERRY We think nearly everyone must know the Royal Family by sight in these days of widespread photographs.

PUCK The arm that a gentleman gives to a lady is not invariably the same; it depends on circumstances of position. We write for girls, not men, and you are too young to think of such things.

UNE PETITE FEMME Take off the feather trimming, brush your matelesse mantle well, and where it is short in the back, put in a square deep black satin kilting, so as to make the back as deep as the front. Then add a small satin-pointed hood at the back, and satin cuffs. You may then add bands of fur or replace the feather trimming.

URSULA Arrasene work is not the same as crewel; the material is a kind of woollen chenille. Of course you should remove your gloves as soon as you sit down to dinner.

A WHITE MOSS ROSE writes a legible hand, and to keep it ladylike she must beware of flourishes.

BRUNETTE We should consider a net unnecessary at night.

STEPHANOTIS The cigar-boxes may be covered with pressed leaves and varnished, or made into coral boxes by gumming rice all over them, and then making a varnish of red sealing-wax, dissolved in spirits of wine, and applied with a brush four or five times successively.

LADY LONG A woman has no right, even by payment, to use a crest. She may only use a lozenge; that is, the family coat of arms in a lozenge, instead of on a shield, but then she must pay tax for using it. She may adopt any fancy motto or device she pleases without tax.

BIG GIRL No one wears long dresses now, but yours should reach the ankles. You should write copies to improve your writing, and never mind if people do think you 'ugly'. Do you remember the story of the 'Ugly Duckling'?

F.E.C. We cannot recommend a depilatory, as they are of little use, we think.

GLORIANNA The initials 'M or N' have been variously explained. It is probable, however, that as we derive much from the Roman Breviary, they mean Mary and Nicholas, the patron saints of boys and girls.

ANEMONE Try glycerine for your sister's head. If too strong, mix with water; it will probably do good.

LOVER OF PEACE wishes us to give her advice, but states her case in rather a mystifying way: 'What remedy would you prescribe for a sister to take to prevent her brother teasing her?' We think it seems as if the brother should have the remedy prescribed for him instead of for the sister, but doubt whether the mischievous little tormentor would take it. We should recommend the sister to assume an appearance of perfect indifference to any annoyance intended.

CHIMBORAZO Whatever the origin of the rhyme may be, the name 'Taffy' as applied to Welshmen has no disparaging meaning, being the familiar form of David Davy, which in Welsh becomes Taffid Taffy.

JET Ladies do not open doors for gentlemen.

CHATTERBOX There is scarcely any difference now made between a hat and a bonnet.

AN EARNEST ENQUIRER writes: 'I have heard it said that if you take a guinea-pig up by its tail its eyes will drop out; but as it has no tail, how can its eyes drop out?' Are you 'earnestly inquiring' for the purpose of testing the result? If you put a little salt on a sparrow's tail, you will be enabled to catch him. 'Earnestly' try the experiment with the sparrow; do as you like about the guinea-pig.

DELICATE PRIMROSE The address of the Seashell Mission is The Secretary, 24 Richmond Terrace, Clapham Road, Kennington, SW; 1,600 boxes have been distributed, and the secretary is anxious to obtain funds to procure suitable boxes for the shells supplied.

DAISY Your letters should be addressed to the care of your host, of course; but not using the expression c/o, which is a commercial abbreviation, and quite vulgar for private use.

DORCAS Endeavour to remove the fruit from the stones with your fork, otherwise remove from the mouth in the hollow of the almost closed left hand, placing it close to the mouth so as to conceal the passage of the stone from the mouth. Never remove them in a spoon.

MAB The cause of the death of your 'table-plants' may probably be traced to lighting your room with gas. You appear to write with a badly cut quill pen, so we can scarcely judge of your writing.

COLUMBINE Dresden is famous for its resources, and we believe Hanover likewise, at which latter place the best

German is spoken. We think that you have quite forgotten yourself; the style of your letter is so unseemly, and contrasts most unfavourably with the grateful, modest, and ladylike tone of the majority of our young correspondents.

ELAINE A thick dress, such as a tweed, is best suited to a tricycle. It should be made like a riding habit, close-fitting, and very neat. Wear black lace round your neck.

PEARL If your hands be too small to stretch an octave, what do you expect us to recommend? We cannot supply a new pair. Perhaps they may grow, as you are still so young.

TOX On the Tweedside, 'kettle' means a social party met together to take tea from the same 'kettle'. If you remember the shape of the instrument called the 'kettle-drum', which was like half an orange, supported on two legs, you will see the reason of the additional 'drum', a word which has for many years signified a crowded evening entertainment, and in that sense is derived from the close packing of a drum of figs.

FEATHERS The disagreeable sensations you hear in your head and ears while singing are due to general weakness of the nervous system. Get two little bottles or phials, one containing diluted phosphoric acid, the other tincture of iron, and take ten drops of each in half a wineglassful of water three times a day. This for a month, then a quinine mixture. Drink only very weak tea, but use cocoa and cream. Take exercise, fresh air, and the bath. Yes, thousands are afflicted like you, only worse. Do not strain the voice. We do not charge for giving advice. It is a real pleasure for us to know that we do our readers good.

VENESSA We do not quite understand what 'an evening concert for the hair' is; and we do not attempt to offer a suggestion as to the alteration of a dress which you do not describe to us.

MINNIE R. We are glad that you took courage to write to us, as you are so good as to say from 'seeing our kind patience with others'. We shall always be pleased to hear from, and counsel you.

MABEL BESSIE The white brilliant dress with two flounces on a kilted skirt, and a polonaise trimmed with Swiss embroidery, would be very suitable for your purpose.

DOROTHY LASCELLES You are ill from overwork and worry, and you are tall for your years. We must tell you the truth: *rest* is the principal thing to cure you. Tonics might prop you up a bit, and a roborant plaster on the loins will help you. Take good food, but nothing to make you sleep. That would be dangerous: also try a bath in the morning.

M. EALKY The double knitting of knees is always a rather clumsy affair. Decide upon the spot in your stocking where the knee will come, and with an extra thread, either of the exact or half size, a silk strand or mending angola, knit the allotted stitches, and with the single thread, continue the round, leaving the extra wool inside. A neater way perhaps, is to run at the back of the knitting with double wool, passing over three and under one. Knit as in some of the gentlemen's gloves.

C. SYKES The passage to which you refer will be found at St. Luke 19: 41. We do not approve of your inquiring where certain texts are to be found. The Holy Scriptures should be studied by our readers themselves so thoroughly that they might be able to answer such questions rather than need to ask them. See St. John 5: 39.

MOSS ROSE Stop plucking the hair from your chin. All will come right in time.

DAY-DREAM Your writing is good but no better than it should be, for, with the advantages of having a governess to yourself, you ought to be a superior girl in everything. That you have yet to learn English is shown by your writing 'Will you please give a pattern of how to make a woollen man's glove in your paper?' We are not so well acquainted with the requirements of woollen men as we are with those of careless and boasting girls.

VIXEN *Noblesse oblige* is a French proverb, and means that nobility of blood and high standing in society lay the individual so circumstanced under an obligation to act in a manner becoming to such a position and antecedents.

JOAN The cage for white mice should be long enough to be divided into two compartments — one for sleeping in and one for the daytime. Feed with bread, cheese, nuts etc.

THEODOSIA We do not consider it at all seemly that any young girls should be out alone at night, even coming from church.

ZOOPHYTE You would be able, with strict economy, and an acquaintance with dressmaking, combined with quick and notable fingers, to dress on £15 per annum. But then you must be wise in the selection of dresses that will wear well, and in the way of making up old ones with additions of other materials, and a change in the style of make. £20 would, of course, render the question of suitable dress one of less difficulty.

A QUILLE PENNE Sleeplessness is always a serious matter in young or old. We expect you are too much confined during the day. We can hardly prescribe, as you do not tell us how you live, eat, work etc. You may write again; meanwhile try three grains of the citrate of iron and quinine thrice daily, and get cod liver oil; buy it from the fish shops, you can in Edinburgh, where you live; it is pure, and good, and cheap. A dessertspoonful gradually increased to a tablespoonful three times a day after food is the dose.

GIGLAMPS There is no harm in you driving in a cab with another lady.

CARP Redness of the nose, though sometimes arising from indigestion, is often caused by cold feet and a lack of proper underclothing. Wear flannels next the skin and woollen stockings, and keep yourself as warm as possible. Avoid anything indigestible.

DEMOISELLE (1) Yes, the morning tub is sure to do you good, if you do not feel the shock too much. (2) Please to repeat this query and tell us what you mean by 'bones growing out of the back'.

MATTIE There is a Convalescent Home at Crescent House, Marine Parade, Brighton; terms, 7s. to 10s. 6d. [35p to 52½p] weekly. Application to be made daily to Mrs Marshman, 2 Redcliffe square, SW, before noon.

CLARIBEL We cannot undertake to read letters crossed as yours.* Few of our other correspondents are so regardless of our rules.

CLARINDA We do not know — and do not wish to know — who wrote the morbid lines which you quote. We think you had better consult a doctor, for you are evidently in a very bad state. Your writing is scandalous.

CIGARETTE The roofed entrance gate of a churchyard is called a 'lich-gate'; because it is a shed, or covered spot, designed to shelter the coffin and its bearers while waiting for the clergyman who is to conduct the procession to the church. The word 'lich' is derived from the Saxon '*Lic*', a dead body; the German being *Leich*. Thus, Lichfield, or the field of the dead, was so called after the martyred Christians who perished there.

BUTTERFLY Wash with soap and water, and then white-wash all over, letting the whitewash remain on for some hours, and then rubbing off.

HATTIE For the making of certain leaves and flowers in vegetables moulds are to be procured. These may be supplemented by the use of a knife. Inquire at a first-class ironmonger's.

AGNES D. Boil the lace in soapsuds, having previously wound it round a bottle. Then dip it in coffee.

LITTLE NELL Cricket is not a girl's game, yet it would be unsisterly to refuse to assist in playing privately with your brothers.

---

*Prior to 1840, the year in which nationwide Penny Postage was introduced, a letter was charged according to distance, not weight. To send a single letter from London to Edinburgh cost 1s. 1½d., and a 'single' letter meant one sheet of paper folded, addressed and sealed without an envelope. If a second sheet or an envelope was used *double* postage was charged.

Since a vast number of the lower paid earned no more for a day's work than the cost of one such single letter, few letters were sent long distances except by the wealthy.

Among the ways of economising on postage was the practice of 'crossing' letters — writing both horizontally and vertically on the same side of the same sheet, which made it very difficult to read. There was no advantage in this from 1840 onwards (see the reply to TENNYSON on p. 50), since several sheets of paper in an envelope travelled for a penny, but some people continued it, probably as an affectation.

KILLICK We cannot promise either articles or illustrations. Look for the word 'oblidge' in your dictionary.

A SCOTCH GIRL is informed that she can get the Index to Vol. I, for one penny [½p], or the Frontispieces to the monthly parts and Index for ninepence [3½p], and the beautiful cloth case, in many colours, for two shillings [10p]. Her bookbinder will put the book together at very little cost.

CURIOUS JANE Do you really believe we would say your handwriting was 'pretty' if it were not? We credit ourselves with candour in these pages, and our columns would not be trustworthy if we were given to flattery. Your handwriting is *not* pretty. There! but you may improve it by patient practice in copying.

CROOKS AND CRANKS Make your bathing dresses of the striped galatea, and bind them with red.

MARY ELLEN Clean your silver jewellery with borax and water. Leave the canary's cage as it is.

KATRINCHA The option rests, not with you, but with your affianced husband, to whom you have been engaged for four years, having assured him that you cared for no one else. You have confessed your change of feeling to him from no fault of his, nor alteration of your mutual circumstances. If he choose to keep one so faithless to her plighted word, she is bound in honour to abide by it.

KEZIAH As we do not know what your proportions are, we cannot tell you whether they would be likely to break a pony's back, or whether your fairy form would suit a small, better than a large, horse.

AMELIA Your friend should use a 'flesh-brush', employing it gently at first, until able to bear a good scrubbing daily, all over the whole person, and especially the feet and arms. She should wear merino or flannel underclothing and stockings, and eat more 'heat-creating' food, such as butter, fat, suet, honey, sugar, treacle, peas, lentils etc, and take exercise indoors, such as skipping, playing battledore and shuttlecock, and in every way that she can accomplish it. She should use a good rough Turkish bath-sheet after her morning's bath, and make the drying a very quick process, as well as the ablutions.

ORPHEUS Workhouse sheeting forms an excellent costume for lawn tennis, and is inexpensive, and easily decorated with embroidery or a coloured trimming, such as Turkey-red twill.

CLARICE There is no certain cure for cold in the head. Camphor is recommended by some, while others have faith in the old-fashioned remedy of putting the feet in hot water and rubbing the nose with tallow, though it is not easy to get a candle of that material in every house now. A cold will generally run its course. Staying in bed and keeping up perspiration will give most chance of checking a catarrh. In summer it is too common a complaint, owing to want of caution. A chill after being heated may begin an illness ending in fever or in consumption. Last year we knew of the death of a bright girl, who caught cold from staying too long out at a garden party. Crowded rooms and draughty doorways are also places where colds lie in wait for you. Don't be ashamed of wrappers.

ALLIE If you care for your soul's health, avoid the novels which you refer to. The writer is one of a set of authors who write books to sell, not to benefit the readers.

TOPSY We are glad that you have found *The Girl's Own Paper* such a help, but we cannot tell you of anyone who would sell their set of numbers cheaply. We hope no girl would esteem the magazine so lightly as to wish to part with her numbers. You can buy the volume beautifully bound for six shillings [30p], the cheapest book in the market, 'although we say it as shouldn't'.

HOPAGOG Put in some cloves to flavour and colour the peas, but if not deep and rich enough in colour, add a little cochineal to the syrup.

EUDORA Not knowing where Barbuda is we cannot give you information. You may be muddling up Bermuda and Barbadoes together.

CONSTANCE GRAY 'Mittens can be worn, instead of gloves, out of doors in the summer.' Of course, if you have no objection to brown, coarse-looking hands.

ELEINKY Girls are not, as a rule, sufficiently educated to be introduced into society until the age of eighteen. Whether any, or the whole, of that education should be accomplished at school is a separate question, and must depend on the circumstances and the personal opinion of the parents.

PINK MAY Veils are most worn, but to many (servants for instance) caps are more suitable.

CLEMENCE TAYLOR You suffer from a bad circulation, produced either by insufficient clothing and food or those which are not suitable for your case, or else from too sedentary a life; or, again, you may have a feeble heart. Take exercise; use a flesh-brush; eat warming food, such as lentils, beans, peas, and so forth; and wear merino under-vests and warm stockings. If not sufficient to improve your state, consult a doctor.

AN ARTIST'S DAUGHTER Your writing covers a good deal of space, and if you ever write a book we fancy you will require a special train to convey the manuscript.

CORAL NECKLACE Gooseberries are not served as a dish for dessert in society. At home, you hold the gooseberry, and having pulled off the little terminal tuft at the end you squeeze the contents into your mouth. In reference to grapes, which always appear at dinners in society, there is a fully acknowledged difficulty. It is a safe rule to notice what the best bred persons do who are present at table with you; but it is an undoubted fact that they usually make a cup of the left hand, place it close to the mouth, and so receive the stones and skins, and convey them as privately as possible to the plate, while others swallow the whole in preference. But no one likes to do either; and the best plan is to restrict your indulgence in all such fruits to private dinners.

DUNELM Wait for five years. What is done in haste will be repented of at leisure.

LOCHGARRON To play the flute is quite as suitable for girls as playing the violin, and in appearance more graceful. Good recitation is more likely to give pleasure than either, being a talent more often available.

ELSINORE In a household comprising a master, mistress and two servants it might suffice to begin with six pairs of best sheets, four of servants' do., twelve best pillow cases and six servants'. Of towels, rough, coarse and fine, twelve each, and twelve for the servants; of tablecloths, for breakfast and dinner, twelve each; of table napkins, large and small to match, twelve each; of pantry cloths, for glass and tea, twelve each and the same for dusters; of pudding do., kitchen and chamber do., twelve each.

LENT LILY We advise you to wear your hair short for a time, as it may serve to strengthen it. Certainly it is by no means 'morally wrong' to wear it thus. In reference to the passage you quote, we believe it only stated the existing feeling of the time as to a style which was not regarded as seemly and womanly. In the present day people are more free to choose fashions for themselves; yet cropped heads are very exceptionally seen in the upper ranks of society.

FORGET-ME-NOT We fear we cannot tell you the value of your coin, as you give no clue to what it is like, nor whether it is of copper or silver. We hope you are a very little girl indeed, for you spell 'writing' with a double 't'.

DAMASK ROSE We have received a long illegible letter from you, which we *think* is sent to inform us that we have not answered previous letters sent by you. We suppose that they were equally badly written, and so received the fate of being instantly destroyed, or that we had others worthier of the space.

TED A girl is not supposed to be out of the schoolroom till after eighteen years of age.

HOPE From the results which you experience after sea bathing, it is evident that it is quite unsuitable for you, and the heart has not sufficient power. Even were we duly 'licensed to kill', we should not prescribe for individual cases without personal acquaintance with them. The best and latest medical works limit the sea bath to a plunge in and out for some, a five minutes swim for others, and ten only for those who can come out of the water in a glow of heat. The amount of reaction is the only reliable criterion for your guidance.

RITA Wear black silk and white lace, and, if possible, a bonnet with violets and white lace. Never cast any shadow of your own gloom on others. It is selfish, or at least thoughtless, to do so. Wear lavender-coloured gloves, and take them off at the breakfast.

UNCAS Those spots which appear on kid gloves, produced by damp, cannot be removed except by re-dyeing, as the colour has been taken out of the part so mildewed. See answer about special curing of bacon shortly forthcoming.

MY FANNY AND G Provided that the friends who give you such nice presents be not gentlemen, you may receive them graciously and thankfully. To return them would indeed be most rude and ungrateful. Have you no albums to show your friends? Or, could you not institute 'Bee Meetings', and all work at some patchwork quilt for the poor, while the rest of the party take it in turns to sing, play, or read aloud?

EVANGELINE Washing the head is said to make the hair grow, but you should not try it unless quite certain not to take cold.

LIZZIE Your nice letter has greatly interested us. You can exercise an influence upon your poor father for good if you like by reading to him from the Bible, by interesting him in your *Girl's Own Paper* and getting him to read it, and by your own example. Go to work in a delicate manner to reform him, for he naturally would resent being preached at by his own child. Cannot you be of service to your step-mother also? For as you are not at home, a great deal of your father's time must be spent in her company. Pray for his reformation and ask God to give you strength and wisdom.

DISAPPOINTED Your best way is to consult a surgeon, who will advise a bandage, or some method of keeping the bone in its place.

FRANCESCA We content ourselves with informing our other readers of the question with which you have thought it worth while to trouble us — 'How tall is Signor Foli?'

MAIDEN HAIR Your Tudor bedstead, which you say has been already painted, might be made very handsome by means of good 'decorative panel painting'; but to paste pictures over it, in patchwork screen fashion, would be in very bad taste.

WREATH OF SMOKE We think the reading of sensational stories very bad for the mind, as they enervate and weaken it.

MISS CHEEKY The licence which you appear to have conceded to your male acquaintances cannot, surely, have existed with the knowledge of your mother or guardian? If people 'consider you fast' it means they consider you hold your reputation for modesty at a very low rate. We refrain from making further quotations from a letter containing confessions which you should have blushed in writing. Remember that a woman's good name and honour are precious treasures, to be accounted for to God, and preserved, if it were even at the cost of life itself. Besides which you have a sacred duty to perform to others, in the blameless example which it should be your life-long effort to set by the aid of Divine grace. Your professing not to be religious (as some appear to boast) is no excuse for unmaidenly conduct.

JUDY Perhaps onions.

TIBBIE Take pains to stand very straightly on both feet. Rub the weaker side thoroughly with unsalted lard once a day, and use sea-salt baths. You are so young you will probably grow out of it.

PERPLEXED HOUSEKEEPER You cannot do better than buy one of the fashionable Persian rugs for the front of the piano; they are thick and soft, rich-looking, and the colours harmonise with everything. Some are very inexpensive; a large one may be bought from 12s. 6d [62½p].

MADGE MUFF The coin is only a penny sewn up in a black ribbon bandage. Consult a surgeon, however, as a lotion might be of use.

CAPRICCIOSO Half an ounce of oxalic acid dissolved in half a pint of water, may probably help you. Try rubbing it first with a piece of India-rubber.

ADA THOMPSON Replace the worn-out silk in your piano-front with a piece of black cotton-backed satin, which you might paint or embroider. You might tone down the red colour of your room by introducing a black screen, or dark curtains and portière.

HUMBLE BEE Rice, sago, hominy, batter and 'hasty puddings' are all suitable for boys, and are inexpensive and easily made.

TORFRIDA It is not only usual, but quite necessary, for a grown-up person to remain in the room while the masters on different subjects are giving their lessons. It ensures the attention of the pupil, and prevents useless conversation.

PROMPT The lining naturally gives strength to the bell-pull, so you may choose any material to work upon suitable to your room. We have just seen a very handsome one of black satin, with a graceful trailing design of Virginia creeper on it. In order to give an opinion we should know for what room it is intended.

JESSIKA Velvet is worn in mourning, but not in the early stages, when it is quite inadmissible.

JANIE, E.E.M., LILLIAN B. and all other Girls who have sent us Christmas Cards and Kind Messages. We thank you heartily for your cheering tokens of friendship and goodwill. It is just a year since the first number of *The Girl's Own Paper* was sent out into the world, and we are heartily thankful to be able to say that the support received has far exceeded the most sanguine expectations of the publishers. The Editor is delighted to inform his readers that the tone of their letters (over 1,000 weekly) has greatly improved, and he is certain that the girls are being led to feel that the aim of life should be high, and that it is far nobler to work hard than to fritter time away in trifling occupations or frivolous amusements. A spirit of modesty and earnestness is the prevailing tone of the letters from our girls. May they ever continue to cultivate these virtues. While acknowledging their kind support and encouraging friendliness which has prompted the sending of the cards, the Editor wishes one and all 'A Happy New Year'.

CLARA PEGOTTY To preserve clothes from dust in drying during winter, have as little dust about as is practicable. Before the linen is hung on the lines or rails, see that the hearth is clean swept; all dust blown from the grate and bars, and the fire itself well replenished and bright. Attend well to the drying. Remove each article as soon as it is ready, and have a clean towel or dust sheet to throw over the increasing pile of dried clothes as you lay them on the folding table.

BLENDONI Skim milk is used, not new. Pour it all over the drawing, and then hang it over the back of a chair to drip dry. Your writing is too formal to be pretty, especially the 't's', which are ugly in the extreme.

VIOLA Very ancient violins by a first-rate celebrated maker are more valuable than new ones, provided they be in good repair. Modern ones may be had from a pound upwards to a high price.

MAL AUX DENTS Whatever tends to strengthen the body and nerves and the system generally, will help to remove the tendency to toothache. Good food, exercise in the open air, quinine and cod-liver oil should be tried. The exercise should be of a pleasurable kind. Use simple camphorated chalk as tooth powder.

BEATRICE Because you have been seven years in your situation you wish to change. You had better think twice and oftener about it. There are hundreds and thousands who would gladly take your place if you left it.

JUNETTA We cannot possibly remember why we did not answer your previous letters.

SISTER CHRISTIAN The Children's Hospital, Great Ormond Street, trains lady pupils from twenty-one to thirty-five years of age at one guinea per week. Write to the matron for further information. Lady-pupils and probationers pay, as a rule, for their training, board and lodging. 'Nurses' are not ladies, and are paid for their services from the time they enter. They are expected to remain in the service of the institution for a certain period after training, each hospital having its own rules. Lady nurses are always called 'sisters'.

MURIEL When at the service you should wear white if possible instead of black. The simpler the costume the better, personal mourning being dropped for the occasion. Many dear girls have sent us bright and pretty Christmas and New Year's cards in a black-bordered envelope. This is a mistake. We do not like the suggestion of a shadow thrown across our path.

LILIAS BERTRAM Could you not sit on a low chair to a table and do the tailoring on it, instead of on your knees? Keep the chair so close to the table that you can rest your very long back always against it, as irritation of the spine might result from such a continual strain upon it.

ROWAN The allowance for each servant per week is a quarter of a pound of tea, half a pound of sugar, half a pound of butter, half a pound of cheese. The rules for work may be written out by any mistress for herself. One room well cleaned each day, so that each room of the house is cleaned once a fortnight. Friday, plate cleaning; Thursday, staircase; Saturday, kitchens, areas and passages downstairs. Keep the sides well washed, but do not whiten them.

PANSIE We cannot make out whether you ask about white pussies or puppies. If they want cleaning, you are better without such pets.

LITTLE IGNORANT French merino would be more durable for the baby's cloak than cashmere. White, trimmed with white, would be suitable. For a long one with a deep cape, it would take about five or six yards of double width. But you should procure a pattern, decide on the length you desire it to be, and then measure the quantity.

AMPHION You can get the information you want at any music shop. If you have no older friend to inquire for you, do not be afraid to ask. A girl of thirteen will be courteously attended to, if they do not happen to be busy at the moment.

A WEAK HEART An article will be given shortly about Married Women's Property. Some changes in the present law are proposed, and you had better wait till the result is known. One thing you may be told now, that any money lodged in the Post Office Savings Bank cannot be taken out without your husband's written signature, and whatever is bought with your savings is his, not yours, by law.

BLUE DOT Damp does not cause worm-eating in a table. The wood must be bad. Ask an upholsterer or carpenter to examine it.

BELLA Soft soap is what is employed for washing dogs, not human hair. We are not acquainted with 'black soap'.

SENSITIVE WHITE ROSE People of really good breeding never leave out the 'Miss' before the Christian name on the visiting card. Boys of twelve or thirteen usually have the prefix 'Master' before their Christian names on letters etc.

EUDORA An apology and a confession must be made. In reply to an inquiry about Barbuda it was said that the Editor did not know such a place, and suggested that Bermuda and Barbadoes had been muddled up together. He ought not to have trusted to memory, but to have consulted a reference book. Barbuda is one of the Windward Islands in the West Indies. Its area is about seventy-five square miles; about fifteen miles long, and eight broad. It lies twenty-seven miles north of Antigua. Corn, cotton, spices, and tobacco are grown there, but not sugar. The island is fertile and well wooded, the forests abounding with game and deer. We thank correspondents who have kindly pointed out the error.

ADA ANNIE Rosemary tea is an old and excellent remedy for falling hair, and costs less than anything we can recommend to you.

SIMPLE SIMON Perhaps glue would fasten the shells more securely than gum. Your writing is very ugly, and 'truely' is not spelt with an 'e'.

AUNT ELLEN Braces are recommended by some people, or the use of a back-board for a certain time every day. If the back be weak, bathe with sea salt and water every morning.

TINY Send the plush to a cleaner. Mantles, visites, and mantillas will be worn this year, and tailor-made jackets — not dolmans. Large hats, and those called 'toques', will be much worn this summer. You may wear a polonaise, and wear it fastened either in front or behind.

JAPONICA The tar may be removed by butter, and the butter by turpentine or French chalk, or by holding a red-hot poker near the grease. We feel shocked by the evil and censorious spirit which you manifest towards your three elder sisters. Before you attempt to make them better, learn not to do worse yourself by sitting in judgement on others.

GIRLIE We were greatly pleased by your letter, which was unexceptionable in its tone, spelling, grammar, and writing. The latter might be copied with advantage by many of our correspondents, who enjoy far greater educational advantages.

MYRA We decline to inform anybody 'the size their waist ought to be'.

POPSEY We have just given full instructions to another correspondent about to be married respecting the house linen that may be required. As to materials, that for the table should be damask linen, more or less fine; the sheets either of linen or calico, or perhaps linen for the top and calico for the under sheets; and calico sheets and pillow cases for the servants' beds. Huckaback and Russian diaper for the towels, and some Turkish bath towels. Linen for the best pillow cases.

VINETTA The autumn is the time for cutting branches off a myrtle tree. We advise you to send it out of the room when the gas is lit.

FAILSWORTH Second word illegible, which is sufficient answer as to handwriting, of which the first requisite is to be easily read. Wear jet, if anything, but all such ornaments are disliked by the most sensible people. Savages wear nose-rings and lip-rings as well as ear-rings.

CRAM There is no objection to the use of a tricycle by ladies in the country, more especially to those that are large enough for two persons.

NETTA There are some small penny books of instruction in French and German sold at every railway station, which we think you will find exactly what you want.

GENTIAN How very dirty the iron pan must be in which you boil the linen! Employ someone to clean it. The 'thick black scum' which you say 'boils off' it, may perhaps be extracted from the clothes, but we are disposed to think and hope that the fault lies with the individual whose business it is to scour the boiler.

MYRTLE By 'cruel' we suppose you mean 'crewel'. Crewel embroidered dresses are always worn.

IDONEAL SCHEAL appears to have rather original ideas of what is 'rude'. It could not be 'rude' for one lady to take the arm of another when out walking. But they should speak low, and look as quiet and sedate as possible.

BEE Call your puppy Gustave or Bruno.

DARWIN It would take too much space to reply here. In general, we may say that Mr. Darwin denies the existence of species, as so made by a Creator, but thinks that all kinds of plants and animals develop themselves, through force of natural influences (as climate, food, and so on) during countless ages of time, till they assume their existing appearance; so that man, by the Darwinian theory, is only a developed ape, and the ape is developed from something less organised, till we get back to the earliest living monad. When the first stone got its life Darwinism leaves to conjecture. The theory is not necessarily atheistic, but it is all sheer nonsense.

MARA If your chintz bed-furniture be worth it send it to a proper person to be calendered, and do not spoil it by attempting to do it at home. Your father must hold the Queen's commission to be entitled to give his servant a cockade.

WILD THYME You are indeed a young housekeeper, but your education has evidently not been neglected, and your writing and composition are so good that they might be shown as an example to many older people. Try a melon-shaped smoking cap in six or eight pieces, each ornamented; or crochet one in the shape of a Neapolitan fisherman's cap, like those which fill the windows of the hatters just now.

AZILI A girl must take the arm offered. The left arm is right usually, but there may be architectural reasons for varying the usage. It might be awkward on a companion ladder or a cork-screw staircase.

A.S. We cannot recommend face powders.

COURTENAY The pillows of a bed should be covered in the daytime with the quilt, and if the bed be an old-fashioned four-poster, the curtains at the head of the bed should be folded and laid across them, with the ends meeting in the middle.

BESSIE Among the French works suitable for young girls, we may suggest Madame de Genlis' *Veillées du Chateau;* the poetical works of Lamartine and his *Voyage en Orient;* and the *Cours d'Histoire*, by Lamé Fleury. All these may safely be put into their hands for educational purposes.

JENNIE WREN Your natural hand, No. 1, is by far the best of the collection, and very good. Your verses very much the reverse.

ROSY AND MATILDA It would be cheapest to purchase the Jersey bodice ready-made. For girls of fifteen they should button at the back.

JENNY GEDDES It is more usual amongst persons in good society to pronounce the word 'spa' as if written 'spaw', than as the 'a' is sounded in 'papa'.

LINNET It is a good plan to talk to the parrot when placed in a dark room.

ERLINDA We are sorry to hear that you have wasted your time in collecting a million of old postage stamps. Unless for the manufacture of stamp-snakes and tails for kites as toys for children, they are utterly valueless.

FLORENCE PEARSON We never heard of a 'dress ring'. The popular idea is that the third finger of the right hand should wear the 'engagement ring'.

RUTH We received about 200 letters on the day that yours came. If only one minute were taken in opening and looking at each, you can calculate how much time it would require. The time taken in writing replies no one can imagine, and many questions cannot be answered off-hand. Therefore it is not likely we can give time to questions of no general interest, and which could be answered by any person at hand.

HUGIN AND MINN Use enough flour to make them into a stiff paste. We should advise your going to a training school at once.

EILEEN We fear there is no way of making arithmetic 'interesting', and do not think it would be desirable either. The more pains taken with its tables and rules the more satisfactory the progress of the student.

BETH We should advise the old-fashioned back-board; bead bags to hold on the head while walking in the schoolroom and house, and the elastic 'chest-expanders'. Many thanks for your prettily written letter, and its recognition of our efforts.

EUCLID Young girls would not be eligible to be received as hospital nurses. At the age of twenty-five you might be taken in to learn the vocation; but many are the moral and physical requisites in intending nurses.

ANNETTE Gentle exercise will keep you quite as slight as you ought to be. If well in health, you may venture to indulge in the good looks derived from the plumpness natural to it, and to youth.

FAY If you know how to enlarge and how to lessen in knitting, you should not need any recipe to knit a diamond-shaped piece. Your writing is very difficult and tiresome to read, and we trust you will never write a book, in mercy to the publishers and printers.

EDELWEISS An unmarried lady, if young, does not usually tell an unmarried gentleman that 'she is very pleased to have seen him' on any occasion. Write an ordinary note of thanks.

AN INTENSE ONE Whether 'Venetian red' would suit the complexion of the self-styled 'Utter One', who says her friends consider her 'quite *too too*', and whose parents' commonsense 'does not quite fall in with her aesthetic ideas', we cannot tell. A little dumpy girl of 'five feet' could scarcely look well holding a sunflower in her hand —

as she suggests — when 'posing for her photograph'. Were we to give an honest opinion, we should suggest her holding a child's coloured balloon by a string, or else a baby's rattle, and wearing a cap and bells instead of the 'daffodils in her hair'. Go back to your nursery, my dear, for your brains seem not to have hardened, and your head, we fear, is more like an addled egg than anything else at present. You require careful treatment, in diet and general discipline, to restore your brains to a healthy condition.

ALISON Never write thus: '9-6-81'. At first sight we could not imagine what the figures meant. It is altogether commercial, and never should be seen in private correspondence.

NEMO It is impossible to answer thirteen questions, and your ingenuity astonishes us in managing to get them into four sentences, and numbering them 'four'. Pray send a selection. Your allowance is two questions.

ETHEL has 'bunyans', and, judging from her letter, is misty in her ideas of spelling. Buy a dictionary, and inquire for a book called *Pilgrim's Progress*.

KENTISH MAIDEN Turn the jackets, and trim with jet passementerie and black Spanish lace, laid on in rows. Your writing would be pretty if your 't's' were better formed and crossed.

FEE-FO-FUM 'Jolly' is certainly not a ladylike word. 'Pleasant', 'agreeable', 'nice', 'delightful', and 'merry' are all words which might well be substituted for it, and prove more accurately descriptive; for few words are more unsuitably employed than that very word 'jolly'.

INETH An ox-gall, to be obtained at a butcher's, will clean your carpet beautifully. The proportions are one-fourth of ox-gall to three-fourths of cold soft water. Apply to the carpet with a clean flannel, wrung out nearly dry from the mixture; do not make it too wet.

BARBUDA We continue to receive, from remote parts of the world now, corrections of our error about Barbuda. We have confessed our error, and have no doubt been forgiven by 'Eudora'. Once more we return to the subject, having pleasure in stating, on the authority of a West Indian correspondent, that 'Barbuda arrowroot is exceedingly good, and that the island is inhabited by a most hard-working and honest set of negroes, who are much sought after as labourers'. Now we hope we have done full justice to Barbuda, and may hear no more of it.

PLANTAGENET We put your letter with its dozen questions into the wastepaper basket. You doubt our veracity and ask our advice in the same breath, and we think the tone which pervades your letter flippant and impertinent.

CLARISSA We strongly urge you to give up all thought of adopting a profession so especially full of temptation and dangers of all kinds. 'Lead us not into temptation.'

HEADLY If there were burglars outside your house trying to effect an entrance, which plan would you adopt to secure safety, to open all the doors and windows, or to shut them? Treat the lightning in the same way. We do not think much of your wiseacre friend's advice.

GYP E. The tulips should lie completely down.

NERISSA We do not understand your question — 'If I can obtain a book in which is told whose money is in Chancery, and when will it run out?' When what will 'run out' — Chancery, the book or the money? The money probably, but we know no such book.

HOPEFUL Speak to the Protestant pastor, or English chaplain, if there is one near. Your character will be lost for life if you stay; and although not known now, all will come out afterwards. You ought to have asked such questions before going abroad with one who may be a convict for anything you seem to know.

SHEFFIELD The best recipe for cleaning sable and furs in general is to sprinkle them well with hot flour and sand, and brush them well afterwards. Then to beat out the dust with a cane, comb it with a wet comb, and then press with a warm iron. For ermine, plaster of Paris should be employed instead of the flour and sand, but the rest of the process should be similar to that above described.

HAM FRILL Cover the gooseberries with a thin layer of melted tallow, which will prevent any air getting to them.

BUTTERCUP Beware of using cold baths without consulting your own doctor, and judge of your constitution. Many really benefit by a quick sponging with cold water who would be seriously injured by immersion in it. Certainly, with any known weakness of the heart it would be dangerous. Warm baths of five minutes duration, taken before going to bed, you might safely enjoy.

LANGLEY There are so many pretty hats, it is impossible to advise you, as you do not give any particulars; the most useful are those trimmed with black lace, as they are suitable for any event.

LIZZETTA A concertina is a very suitable instrument for a girl, but you must ask permission of your mistress to play it in her house, or else only when the family are out.

ARUM LILY We are sorry to hear that your poor aunt's bequest has tempted you to make a pitiable object of yourself, and a laughing-stock for all sensible people. 'Aesthetic dress' has been scouted almost out of sight, and only appears on the stage in burlesque performances. As to making your hair 'frizzy', we hope you will not succeed. Why should you look like a white negress? Whether 'aesthetic', or ladylike and reasonable, young girls do not require stays. Whalebones in the dress-bodice will keep it from being wrinkled. We advise you to desist from sending off what seem to be rockets from all your 't's'. They look crazy.

BIRDIE Your letter evinces a lack of that delicate feeling of propriety which all girls should possess.

BETSY It would be an impertinence to give a private address, even of a man well known to the public.

ROSS We are at a loss to understand why so many girls are demented on the subject of the natural plumpness which nature bestows on youth. It is a sign of health, unless your doctor have pronounced it to be dropsy in your particular case. And indeed, if you attempted to upset nature's arrangements and to use artificial means for making yourself a scarecrow, dropsy might be a very probable winding up of the little game. Your suggestion respecting the application of vinegar quite shocks us. You little know how ill you soon would be.

MARIA TERESA 'How much chance you have of being an authoress' we do not know; it depends on the number of ideas you possess. The essay you enclose does not contain many, so we do not rob you in consigning it to the fire.

DIMPLED DOTTIE If your friends be out when you call, leave your card with the servant who answers the door. If they be at home, go in, tell the servant your name distinctly, and follow her to the drawing-room. We do not understand your difficulty.

CHARIS In reference to the craze which appears to exist among young people to make themselves thin when nature intended them to be fat, we can only refer you to the answer just given to a fellow-sufferer, who calls herself 'Ross'. Besides, a lean teacher, or governess, is a very unattractive looking object to children. They are always supposed to be cross.

'DISSAPOINTMENT' We do not understand how the young lady so styling herself could be reasonably disappointed that she failed in gaining a prize or even certificate, for her essay at the last competition. Her letter is sufficiently explanatory, as she uses wrong words such as 'a know' instead of 'I know', and a specimen of her spelling may be seen in her adopted name. Besides all this, her writing is a wretched specimen of the art.

MAID OF ATHENS Coal-tar soap is much approved of by many for skin complaints. We cannot, however, prescribe it for you.

ECILA It is generally considered advisable to cut off the hair after severe illness.

SILVER TIP No, wearing earrings can have no effect on the eyesight, either for good or bad. Although many girls wear their engaged ring on the left hand, the orthodox position for it is on the third finger of the right hand.

ELLEN We should know the condition of your wardrobe before suggesting how you should expend the £10 legacy.

If well supplied with summer clothing, and not with winter wraps, remember that July and August are the months in which to purchase furs with economy. A jacket and muff, or deep trimmings for a thick cloth jacket, might prove a valuable purchase. If provided with winter dress, perhaps some of your legacy might be laid out with advantage in under-linen, and in the purchase of boots and shoes, which wear the better for being well seasoned.

TWO ELDER SISTERS The 'creaking' of which you complain is to be attributed partly to lacing too tightly, and also to the circumstance that the whalebones are not well secured in closely fitting casings, and, when damp, they produce a noise like that of some boots and shoes.

HOPEFUL AMATEUR In reference to your desire to go on the stage, we can only say we strongly urge you to abandon the idea. It is a position of terrible danger.

ROSAMOND We cannot advise the use of depilatories, and the use of tweezers is even worse. In some cases the razor must be used, but in your case we should think that much good might be effected by using juniper tar soap and cold water.

A DARK-EYED GIPSY We employ borax and camphor as a wash for the hair ourselves, and see no cause for apprehension that it will turn it grey.

ELDER SISTER No, old postage stamps are of no use, except for the manufacture of 'stamp snakes', which are very nice playthings for children. They require about 4,000 penny stamps for the body alone, while half-penny ones are needed for the tail [until October 1880, half-penny stamps were half-size]. The head is made of black velvet, having bead eyes, but we think that you would require to see one, before you could manufacture one properly yourself.

LALAGE You should have lessons from a swimming mistress. We cannot 'give you a compliment on your writing', nor on your spelling, nor grammar.

LUCY OF ELLANGOWAN For an elderly person we could not recommend more suitable work for leisure moments than strips of knitting or crochet-work, with which to form young children's winter petticoats.

EXPIRING FROG We do not think the information would be of value to anyone, so must decline to give it to you.

DEWDROP A magic-lantern, bright-coloured pictures of places — say in the Holy Land, which can be explained and described — and some music — vocal and instrumental — are all good ways of amusing the poor.

HOPE DALE You must take your own soap when you go on board ship, and we should advise your wearing a veil constantly.

LITTLE GIPSY The decay of your teeth may be owing to your state of health. Flowers of sulphur, used as a tooth-powder once a day, sometimes prove beneficial. Wear loose boots, washing the feet constantly, and keeping the callous parts well rubbed with pumice-stone when under water.

TOPAZ Write to the secretary for the examination papers. Clean with bath brick and finish with a little oil.

ANNA We could not help you in this matter, as we wholly disapprove of Planchette and all kindred amusements.

TEASE OF STRETFORD A little girl of sixteen writes to inquire whether, at that time of life, she should be 'cold and proud', and whether she should 'ponder and screw'. We fail to understand what she does when she performs the operation called 'screwing'. We have heard of 'screwing-in a waist', and hope she does not contemplate any practice so baneful and silly. Let her be gentle, modest, and natural, putting on no airs of any kind. When well in health and kindly cared for, and trying to do her little duties well, she could not be other than lively and gay, instead of, as she expresses it, 'cold and proud'.

LOTTIE Three months is the duration of mourning for a first cousin. You may wear white frilling round your neck.

WHITE PUSSY thinks it worth while to write and inquire 'Do you like lemon? I do. There is another *queston* I forgot.'

SUBSCRIBER You require black or blue tracing paper to transfer your pattern. You surely don't mean to say that you have never taken a bath?

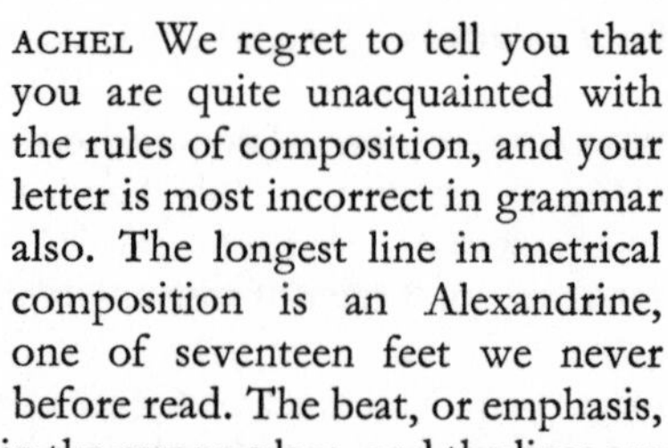

RACHEL We regret to tell you that you are quite unacquainted with the rules of composition, and your letter is most incorrect in grammar also. The longest line in metrical composition is an Alexandrine, one of seventeen feet we never before read. The beat, or emphasis, usually falls in the wrong place, and the lines are quite irregular in length. We do not approve of the very unjust slur cast on the brave men in a higher rank of life, and who, you say, 'would scorn to lend a helping hand, to save from those fiery billows'. The first gentleman in the land, H.R.H. the Prince of Wales, has never 'scorned' so to do, and is himself a fireman!

POCAHONTAS You might make a rustic stand for flower-pots with pieces of stick and cork.

HELEN Get up and walk about the room, allowing the bed to cool. Perhaps you have too many clothes on it or too few over your feet to keep them warm. There is probably some simple reason of this sort.

LOUISE Tea stains are taken out of linen with glycerine. From your letter writing we should think you a gentleman.

COWSLIP Your time is too valuable to be wasted on brooding over little personal ailments and defects. Your spelling, writing, and composition are bad. Try to improve them.

MEERSCHAUM The fourth finger of the left hand is that on which the wedding ring is placed, and the engagement ring, till then usually worn on the right fourth finger, is placed on the same finger. [The Editor was not always consistent, *see* pp. 34, 39 and 48 for other replies on the subject.] But, with the exception of the wedding ring, it is quite immaterial on which finger you wear any other ring.

LALLA The simplest way of coating or polishing plaster of Paris casts is with skimmed milk. Lay it on the model till it will imbibe no more, laying it on with a camel's hair brush. Then place it aside where it will be free from dust. When quite dry it will look like polished marble. If the milk be not perfectly skimmed it will not answer.

QUEEN MAB There is no particular value in Canadian or Chilian stamps, excepting in exchange for others.

A.E. How many more girls are going to ask us to give them particulars of making Everton toffee? We have given it once or twice. Look in the Index of Vol. I, for of course you have got your numbers bound. Whether you have or have not, however, we cannot waste our space by repeating these things.

SYBIL We see nothing to prevent your making a scarf tunic out of the crimson serge, below the jersey, which will completely hide the mark left by the fancy braid. Drape it in long folds at the back.

A.M.B. All requisite directions for the hanging of curtains to a mantelpiece are to be found in Vol. I. The illustration given will show how they are to be held back. They should only just touch the ground, and if your chimney-piece be of marble, you must have a board made to fit upon it, to which the curtains can be attached.

JENNY LIND The sparkling globules you notice are bubbles of fixed air. Such brown spots are caused by washing the face while hot.

COUNTRY BUMPKIN We could not recommend you to dye your skin, like an Indian, unless you mean to take to the woods, and thereby preserve your face from the stings of insects.

TOUJOURS GAI Your canaries should have nourishing food — egg and crushed hempseed — in addition to their ordinary food. When moulting and afterward, if they seem weak, a rusty nail in water will give them a tonic also.

WAPPY We greatly commend your handwriting, which is beautifully regular, and every letter correctly formed.

BUTTER We think you lack determination, or you would cure such an ugly trick.

J.J. Use tweezers and pumice-stone to the chin only.

SWEETHEART Vol 2 of *The Girl's Own Annual* has been bound, and is now on sale. The bindings are of many and varied colours. Some are quite white (for wedding presents), and are sold at the ordinary price of 6s [30p].

BROWN EYES A half-worn cashmere or beige would be a good dress for the voyage; and some kind of a hat with a brim, as you will probably suffer from heat after you leave England. Many ladies supply themselves with a black grenadine, as the only sensible cool dress. As no washing is done on board, you will need plenty of underclothing. Be careful to wear tidy boots and dark stockings, and have plenty of clean lace for your neck. Several pairs of gloves are also needed.

ORIANA Is your letter intended as an impertinence?

PEARL AND RUBY The best material for black petticoats is what is called by drapers Italian cloth, which has a satin-finished face. It wears admirably.

KATE WOLESLEY Half a crown [12½p] a night is the usual price, we believe, for a bedroom in most places. We should advise moving from one place to another.

CETEWAYO It is very easy to procure small heads of plaster on which are marked all the bumps known to phrenology. However, you should beware of rash judgments, as the bump you inquire about *may* be a bone.

QUEENIE wants to know what kind of present she should give to a religious middle-aged person, half lady, half servant. How anyone could be 'half a lady' we cannot tell. She must either be one or not. Poor ladies may have to work in trying ways to earn their bread, but it does not deprive them of their birth and culture. As to the present, consult her appearance. Does she need articles of dress — such as gloves, caps, aprons, or collars? When poor, any such things are acceptable.

ONE WHO WISHES TO IMPROVE By tightening-in a round antimacassar design while working you would be able to make a cover of it.

IRIS Your writing reminds us of Stonehenge, and is ugly in the extreme.

LOT'S WIFE We decline to correspond with anyone who has so little proper feeling and is so flippant as to call herself by such a name. It is quite profane, remembering the awful judgment of God upon the wife of Lot.

LOUIE TRUNDLE Gentlemen's braces are generally worked on silk canvas, and lined with white leather. We have recently seen some very pretty ones in Germany, worked in cross-stitch on the ordinary webbing, ingrain silks and cottons being used.

TOPSEY All Walter Scott's novels are good, but read *Ivanhoe*, it is spirited, and will not make you cry much.

MARGUERITE Mourning for a brother or sister is what is called 'deep mourning', and the skirt must be trimmed with crape, as well as the bodice, jacket, and sleeves. The bonnet is entirely of crape. Jerseys are not considered in good taste when worn in deep mourning.

CORNCRAKE We are much obliged by your offer, but our contributors in all classes of literary and artistic work are so numerous that we think it advisable not to increase them.

LILIAN Shepherds are, it is thought, the original inventors of crochet, and it used to be called 'shepherd's hooking'. The word 'crochet' is from the old Danish *krooke*, French *crochet*, a hook. The art was practiced on the Continent in the sixteenth century, and was then known as 'nun's work'. It was brought into Ireland at an early date, and was then called 'Irish point'. It became a fashionable employment in 1837 or 1838.

AMIENS Mathematics and algebra do not appear to be in your line, and if so thin as you describe, the less you worry yourself over them the better. Give your mind rest, and do not take long walks.

BLUE ROSE Ask your music mistress to speak to your parents on the subject, and if they still desire it, do the best you can to please them. Be assured the best blessings lie in the path of obedience and submission.

VERAX We are very much obliged to you for the recipe you give us for preserving eggs, which we subjoin: 'Collect the eggs before May, not in the summer, because the hens eat cockchafers, which prevent their keeping, but they may also be collected in the autumn. Stand them on the small ends in a high, narrow pan, and cover them with lime made into a thick paste. The making of each separate egg airtight is unnecessary. This is the German method of preserving them.' What a very nice hand you write!

UMBRA Wet the fruit stain, and hold over it a lighted lucifer match, so that the fumes of the sulphur may reach it.

MIGNONETTE A basin of vinegar left on the kitchen floor at night, and sticks laid like ladders round its edges for the beetles to climb up by, is a good thing; they will thus fall over the edge and drown themselves.

TIBBY You are indeed much too young to be engaged to any man. You are not out of the schoolroom, and could not possibly know how your taste will change at mature age. The lad of nineteen should be thinking of his lessons, or his trade. He might prefer you to every other little girl now, and when grown up might laugh at his boyish fancy. His engagement would not be binding in law, because he is a minor. We are shocked at your inquiring whether you may be (what you call) 'engaged', and walk with him 'without the consent of your parents'! They should send you to a boarding school, with a hint to the mistress to watch you.

ALLSHORN You ought to be able to get the 'young donkey about two months old' for from fifteen to twenty-five shillings [75p to £1.25]. The price of donkeys has risen considerably of late years. One could once purchase for ten shillings a donkey that one is now asked thirty shillings for. Almost any outhouse fairly weather-tight will do for a stable.

OIKOS We do not understand the people in the shops being ignorant of 'workhouse sheeting', but should have thought the thick, coarse twilled yellowish cotton material was known to all men. The price is from 1s. to 1s. 2d. [5p to 6p] per yard, we think.

COLLECTOR No farthings are commoner than those of Charles II; you can buy as many as you like for a penny each. The farthing with the young head of George II would sell, according to its condition, for from threepence to sixpence.

CITHERA wishes to know 'whether tea-leaves are good for rabbits or not'. Neither good nor harm, in moderation; but tea-leaves are not British, and rabbits are best fed on the vegetables of their own country.

DEVONSHIRE A washleather dipped in cold water and wrung out, rubbed over the surface, will remove hairs, threads and dust, and will brighten up the carpet.

HARYOT NOLLY Eat buttered toast with a knife and fork, if possible, but you must be guided by the customs of the house.

ZYLTHA We should feel much obliged if you would kindly send us the name of the institution in London which 'requires the collection of a million of stamps before admitting a blind child'. We shall be glad to make enquiries into the subject, as we think you have been misinformed.

ALLIE ALDRIDGE We should consider it right to have false teeth at any age, as a matter of health, to say nothing of appearance. We cannot suggest any other ingredient to render water less hard for making tea than carbonate of soda.

EUTERPE Put a piece of wadding, or soft substance, on the part of your violin pressed by your chin, or else alter the position of the former, and learn to play it when held downwards, reversing the pose of the instrument.

LUCRETIA We cannot think it needful for you to take chlorate of potash every evening. Better to strengthen your general health by means of a tonic, and so increase the power of your voice.

FLOSSIE Your ideas about the sermon case are very good. It is only decorated at one side, and should be lined with silk, but no cardboard is required to make it stiff, as it should be soft enough to put in the pocket easily.

OLIVETTE Use a net for the horse when driving.

LISMORE When you write a letter of condolence to any friend who has lost a relative you should write on paper with a very slight bordering of black; but you should not continue to do so if you are not in mourning yourself.

WILHELMINA ESTELLE We think you have little idea of maidenly propriety when you suggest its being 'the orthodox thing' to go and meet a man at the station who is a stranger to your family, when it would be derogatory to you to meet one who was a friend of the family. The mutual friends at whose house you met the gentleman in question should give him a letter of introduction to your family. But it is utterly unseemly for any girl to meet men at stations, unless engaged to them.

SUNFLOWER 'Sweet be the reflection', 'A day nearer the dawn', 'Clothe also thy soul with prayer', would all be suitable as mottoes for a toilet table.

MONICA Nothing can help you but wearing gloves constantly. Tinted paper is used by everyone, and is considered quite ladylike.

CLEMATIS We strongly advise your having nothing to do with anything so nearly resembling the 'curious arts' mentioned in the Scriptures. Unless you, too, desire 'to hold communion with bad spirits', put Planchette in the nearest fire. [Planchette: a board mounted on two castors and a pencil-point, used as a medium for automatic writing and supposed spirit messages.]

PAUVRETTE The cook must clean the boots, if there be only two servants, and the housemaid the knives.

BRUNSWICK We by no means recommend you to make quilts decorated with postage stamps in 'imitation of patchwork'. You had better make a specimen of real patchwork.

IGNORAMUS If you care to write a polite letter to us, we will with pleasure answer your question.

JESMINE Many girls have written questioning our assertion that the third finger of the right hand is the correct one for the engagement ring. We adhere to our statement as being a right one, and should advise all girls who have used the third finger of the *left* hand for this purpose to reverse the custom at once.

TOMBOY Ask your family doctor. Perhaps a small blister might be of use.

ORPHAN You are very clever to have made your mother's caps for so long a period, but we do not wonder the widow's borders are a great difficulty to you. You will require several round wooden sticks, on which to run the borders when you have hemmed them. Press them very tightly together to make the creases you mention, and then damp them with a little very clean gum-water. After this, stand the sticks, with the borders on them, on a plate in the oven, and bake them for a little time. Only experience will enable you to go through these various procedures in such a delicate way, that the borders will emerge from your hands quite unsoiled. But as you say that you are anxious to 'try and try again', we give you the plainest instructions possible.

IVY You have asked us a lot of absurd questions, which of course we do not intend to answer; but, before consigning your letter to the wastepaper basket we wish to ask you to learn the spelling of the following easy words: raspberry (you had it rasberry), whose (whos), amiss (amis), right (write!). Also we might mention that you mix the singular number with the plural, punctuate in the wrong places, omit capital letters, and write a disgraceful hand. It would be wiser of you to try to improve your education instead of 'reading jollie novels'.

LEELA MAY appears to have peculiar ideas on the subject of propriety and maiden reserve. Unless engaged to a man, and with your parents' consent, you are acting very improperly in walking with any man alone. But if, as you say, you are engaged to another man, and walk with or accept the gifts and attentions of anyone but your affianced husband, your conduct is still more reprehensible, and the man would be quite justified in breaking off the engagement. Your conduct disgraces you.

GREY AND GOLD If you have taken *The Girl's Own Paper* since it first came out, and are 'avidious' readers of it, we do not see how you missed finding an answer to your query about Thomas à Kempis.

MOUSIE We do not recommend soda to wash the hair, as it makes it brittle, dry, and harsh.

PLAYER We do not know that 'an apron is required' at lawn tennis, as many clubs exist which do not adopt them at all. All, however, have some simple, pretty dress, or uniform, in order to be alike. Lawn-tennis pouches are very generally used to contain the balls and bags to hold the shoes worn for playing. The pouches hang at the waist, and are often very beautifully embroidered and decorated.

HESTER Persons exposed to cold or wet during the day should bathe their hands and feet in hot water at night, which will prevent any ill effects. So easy a remedy should not be neglected.

A LONG CROSS PARISHIONER The generally accepted way to spell 'mama' now is with one 'm'. Grey flannel wears well, and keeps its colour better than red.

PUPIL TEACHER If you cannot manage to obtain exercise enough out of doors, you will find battledore and shuttlecock assist you in retaining your health. It is the most invigorating of games, and keeps hands, arms, and shoulders, as well as the back, in easy motion. The Americans have an amusing game called 'beanbags', which is played by three or four people. It merely consists of a few small bags filled with peas or beans, which are thrown rapidly from one player to the other. We can well imagine that, after being in the school all day, you are stiff and chilly, and want something to warm and amuse you as well.

TENNYSON There is no excuse for crossing a letter when an ounce of paper goes by post for a penny.

CARRIE To wear short hair curled across a low forehead is certainly not becoming. It gives a low type of expression to the countenance, and spoils the proportions of the face.

LILY OF THE VALLEY The best method for sweetening meat when tainted, either through forgetfulness or soft weather, is to put a few pieces of charcoal, each about the size of an egg, into the pot or saucepan with the meat or fish to be boiled.

AMY Yes.

NIGHTCAP Washing materials are the most suitable for bed-satchels. The pocket may be partly completed before being sewn on the satchel; the embroidery can then be completed over the joinings.

MARIANA A handful of figleaves, boiled in two quarts of water until reduced to a pint, will remove stains from bombazines, cloth, crape etc, a sponge being dipped in the decoction, and the dress carefully and gently rubbed with it.

NELL Owing to the durability of crewel-work, the convenience of being able to wash it, and the interest connected with it as an ancient style of work — applicable alike to furniture and wearing apparel — it is not likely ever to be wholly laid aside; more especially by those whose artistic taste and knowledge of drawing contribute the additional pleasure to the work of designing patterns for themselves.

BOADICEA The celebrated lotion for the hair of Dr. Erasmus Wilson is the best.

FLORRIE The dress for skating should be short enough, so that it should not interfere with the motion of your feet. You should be most careful to wrap up warmly, as few English girls do so. Wear flannel knickerbockers.

IOTA Exercise and the avoidance of the flesh-forming foods and milk would tend to reduce a tendency to grow excessively fat. But remember that it is always a dangerous experiment to endeavour to reduce flesh, even under a doctor's suggestions.

CREWEL WORKER Miss Linwood made copies of the old masters in needlework. She copied the beautiful 'Salvator Mundi' of Carlo Dolce, and was offered £5,000 for it. We do not know where you could see a specimen of her work just now, but will inquire.

PRIMULA Eruptions on the face arise from various causes; a bad digestion, unwholesome food, swallowing food too quickly before half masticated, employing the brain too soon after meals (which should never be set at work while the stomach is engaged), stooping the head at any employment after meals, poorness of blood from insufficient or low diet, eating too many sweet things (causing acidity), intemperance, or, lastly, not using good soap, once a day, in washing the face. A soap having as little alkali as possible is best.

PAPA'S PET You may knit a pair of muffatees as follows: cast on 68 stitches, and knit like a stocking, in a pattern of two plain, and two purl alternately. They may be as long as you like. Then finish them with a crochet edge of several rounds of double crochet, making a chain of three stitches and missing three.

LADY ANNA What do you mean by 'Will my writing do?' Do what — walk, talk or laugh?

TOTTIE You have not read our instructions for tracing with the least attention; they could not be more plainly expressed. Tracing-paper is to be purchased by the sheet at any stationer's, and is asked for under that name. 'Powdered charcoal, and chalk' mean those materials in the form of powder. You have expressed yourself in such a way as to be almost unintelligible. It seems a question as to whether you speak of powdering the charcoal and chalk or powdering yourself.

LYRA ALVIN Your question is too vague. If exercise be desired, no game is preferable to battledore and shuttlecock. If a sedentary recreation, try the arrangement of a scrap-covered screen.

CONSTANCE MARIE Your spelling, handwriting and composition will certainly bear improvement. We shall probably insert a crochet boot for a baby soon.

EDINA Pray do not put to us such absurd questions. We decline to give advice to love-sick girls.

NETTIE Old postage stamps are of no use. You do not whip your eggs enough, perhaps. Add a little powdered sugar to the whites, which will give a slight stiffening.

POLLIE Two nice warm suits for poor boys of six or seven can be made from an old serge skirt.

MARION Young girls should not wear flowers in the hair. We feel complimented by your liking our paper 'pretty well'. We are so sorry that we cannot in return congratulate you on either your spelling or writing.

ZARA Try to forget yourself and your appearance, and be quite assured that nobody is taking any notice of you.

SYLVIA We shall give some new crochet designs for antimacassars in a week or two. No prizes are offered for this work at present.

FLORA The teeth should be well brushed in the morning with powdered chalk, and at night with Castile soap. They should be brushed with plain water after dinner also.

STUMPS Instructions for making the nightingale will appear shortly.

PRIMROSE A useful mixture for allaying the intense itching caused by chilblains is sulphurous acid three parts and glycerine one part, diluted with the same quantity of water. Apply with a soft camel-hair brush. The general causes are lack of exercise and of warm clothing, and the heating of the surface skin at the fire before the blood has been well circulated inside.

FERN A 'cloud' is a long scarf; were the shape a square, it would be a shawl, or, if small, a handkerchief. Half a yard wide and two yards long are the usual dimensions of a 'cloud'.

MILLY There is no easier way of curling hair than putting it in paper, or rag-pinned.

EVA Weak eyes are common enough in young girls of fair complexion and a somewhat feeble constitution. Weak cold green tea is the best and safest application, but cod liver oil — a dessertspoonful three times a day — often works wonders in such cases. The oil should be gradually increased till a tablespoonful can be taken. Steel drops should also be taken.

FRANK What do you mean by 'straightening yourself'? If you mean that you stoop, the old-fashioned face-board stuck into your belt is the best cure that we can recommend. This can easily be made for it. It is shaped like a battledore with the middle cut out, only of a flat piece of wood.

GINGER A whole ham is rarely seen at table except at breakfast.

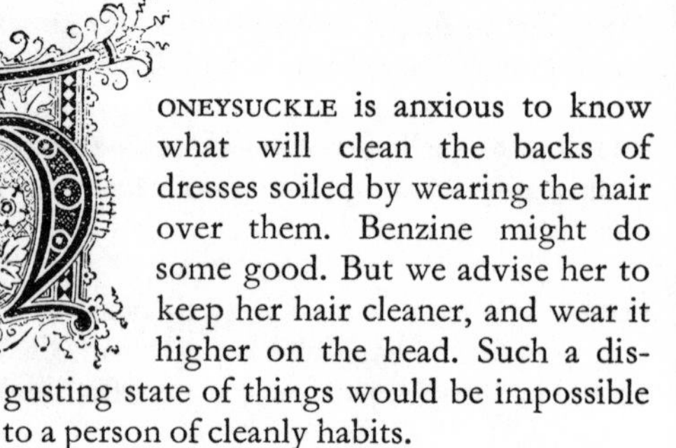

HONEYSUCKLE is anxious to know what will clean the backs of dresses soiled by wearing the hair over them. Benzine might do some good. But we advise her to keep her hair cleaner, and wear it higher on the head. Such a disgusting state of things would be impossible to a person of cleanly habits.

OPHELIA We think there is sufficient liberty in all the fashions of the present day to allow you to wear your own hair as you like it the best, and for everyone else to do the same.

RAG BAG Getting the feet wet is a common cause of toothache. We have heard that using flowers of sulphur as a tooth powder will prevent your being attacked by it.

TOTTLES Make your confirmation dress of white cashmere, or fine white serge, which you could wear in summer for the afternoon. Black boots are worn, not white.

IVANHOE Keep no food in your bedroom and the mice will probably desert it. If you kept a scrap of toasted cheese on your bed, very likely the mice would manage to climb up there, but we do not think they would bite you (as you seem to apprehend) when they had the choice of eating the cheese. We never heard that the bite of a mouse was fatal.

USEFUL To 'make your collar and cuffs look like new' after you have washed them yourself, try stirring the starch when boiling with a wax candle.

WAVIE We never before heard that 'a dark gentleman was the best person to be let in first on New Year's morning'.

FANNY Your enquiry respecting the making of an electric telegraph machine, is so expressed as to be utterly unintelligible. We advise you to devote a little time to learning your English grammar. There is not a single instance of punctuation in your letter. If you wish to manufacture such a machine you should take lessons of some mechanic.

MARTHA The best kind of paper for cutting up for pillows is old letters and envelopes, which are stiff, and have some elasticity in them.

SEABIRD Of course you must abide by the rules on which the competition is offered. It is an evidence of slop-work to make a nightdress without gores. Long-haired beaver hats are more fashionable at present than any others.

DHU We do not give patterns of nightcaps. They are not wholesome, are bad for the hair, and are out of date.

GODIVA The fourth finger of the left hand has from long usage been consecrated to the wedding-ring, from an ancient belief that from it a nerve went direct to the heart. So completely was this fanciful piece of physiology confided in by the Greeks and Romans, that their physicians termed this the medical or healing finger, and used it to stir their mixtures, believing that nothing noxious could communicate with it without its giving immediate warning by a palpitation of the heart.

LILY GREY A buttered biscuit with cayenne pepper sprinkled upon it, or two thin slices of bread and butter so sprinkled, and put together sandwich fashion, will often relieve a bilious headache.

POPPY You wish to have our opinion of your handwriting. We regret to say that it is vulgar, being written sloping backwards; coarse, being two sizes too large; inartistic, having no beauty and grace of form, and decidedly unladylike.

PRACTICAL We can only advise you, as we have recommended others, to endeavour to procure trade orders at shops. We do not think that ladies ever wear crochet edgings, but we have known its sale at a shop, and suppose it was for children's clothing, or the lower classes.

OXFORD DAISY Bathing the eyes with cold green-tea does good sometimes. Do not read small print nor do fine needlework; nor use your eyes much by candlelight, and never sit facing a candle when reading or working.

MARCH HARE Bathing costumes are not made of such heavy materials as they formerly were. Galatea stripes trimmed with red Turkey twill, white or coloured flannel, or a light-made gown of dark blue serge, would be very suitable.

FLAT IRON If really engaged to be married to the gentleman of whom you speak, you may take short walks alone with him; of course with the proviso that you have the consent of your parents or guardians.

ADAH Toothache and a sympathetic ear-ache are produced by some decay in the tooth. Apply a hot poultice of bran to the jaw and ear, or a roasted onion to the latter.

BRIAR The foot which you place on the step of a carriage depends on whether there be a second step to be taken, and on which side you are to take a seat. If there be but one step to make, and you are to sit, for example, on your left side, step on the right foot; if on the right side, use the left foot; if there be two steps to take, reverse these directions.

VERA Netted d'oyleys will shortly appear.

FLOWER POT The best 'recipe for corns' is to wear hard, tight, leather boots; especially those with very pointed toes and high heels.

ELLAND wishes to know 'if first cousins marrage is leagle'! Yes.

MISS CASPAR may be very thankful that she is blessed with such excellent indications of good health as the rosy face and a stout body. She must be very handsome indeed in face, and very unusually elegant in figure and in carriage, to look at all well if thin. A thin little girl is a pitiable sight!

EMMELINE We do not understand what difficulty there can be in re-painting your bedstead.

ENRIQUETA The whole tone of your letter is highly objectionable, and your composition, spelling, and calligraphy need much correction, before you aspire to the publication of any of your 'tales'.

AVRIL The best cure for cold feet is to take good exercise, such as skipping with a rope, and to wear woollen stockings. Of course, your face and nose will be red if your feet be cold. The blood must go somewhere. Going into a warm room, especially if you sit close to the fire, will heat the outer skin, while the flesh is cold inside, and do you harm.

GORDON HAY Perhaps you need more feathers for your screen. It will need a great many. Do not cut off any portion of the fringe of the flues above the eye. The handles can be purchased at any fancy-work shop.

BEATRIX It is not necessary to call in medical advice on the question of your safety in leaving off stays; but your dresses will have to be very carefully made, and well supplied with whalebone, to prevent the bodice from wrinkling and turning up at the waist. You may also need a little warmer lining to them, or an extra covering of some sort.

HYACINTH Do not attempt to 'improve your figure' otherwise than by holding yourself well up, and resting your back when fatigued by lying down on a hard sofa.

SCOTT You do not say whether you want a 'Tam O'Shanter' pence jug cap, or one of full size.

ASHY sends us no less than ten questions in one letter. None of these are commenced with a capital letter, nor a number, nor, indeed, is there a single stop in the whole epistle. Her letter is a deplorable specimen of bad writing, and ignorance of punctuation and grammar.

AUDREY Plenty of photographs of Longfellow are sold in photograph shops, and at stationers. His residence is at Cambridge, Massachusetts, U.S.A.

A READER An excellent jelly for an invalid is made with rice, sago, pearl-barley, and hartshorn shavings, of each one ounce. Simmer with three pints of water, till reduced to one, and strain it. When cold it will be a jelly. Give it — dissolved in milk or broth — in change with other nourishment. Oatmeal jelly is made by allowing the water to remain on the oatmeal over night, and then boiling *the water only;* sweeten and flavour with lemon.

TERPSICHORE Under the treatment you propose to give your floor the varnish will speedily disappear as well as the stain.

DOLLIE Correspondents should select short and uncommon pseudonyms, avoiding 'A Constant Reader', 'A Lover of the G.O.P.', and other such hackneyed phrases. They should also refrain from calling themselves by such flattering names as 'Fair Maid of Perth' etc, and from giving themselves the names of men.

ESTELLE Always pay your own expenses, when you happen to be with any gentleman, merely a friend, or acquaintance.

BLOSSOM It is said that washing in buttermilk whitens the skin; in any case, it is good for the complexion. One of your questions respecting medical treatment is scarcely a delicate one, and we decline to answer it. For what reason do you drink camphor water, if not recommended to do so by a doctor?

TORTESENE Black beads are considered mourning, but gold jewellery with precious stones cannot be worn with any propriety.

MINERVA We do not perceive any suitability in the name 'Madcap' to a tennis club. If you wore any distinguishing uniform you might reasonably call the club the blue, red, green, or black caps. Black and gold would be a well-selected combination for the uniform.

GUERNSEY GIRL Hats are universally worn by young girls of all ages.

MARIETTE No one takes off either hats or bonnets at a wedding breakfast.

ZARA DE BONGE You know how to make a great many mistakes in spelling in a very short letter. Try to do better next time you write.

VERENA No one should wear a long dress at present, whether young or old, excepting in evening and full-dress costume. The dress of a girl of fifteen should be of a convenient walking length, just clearing the ground.

ZOE Of course, laurel and ivy leaves are not suitable food for rabbits.

FROGGIE It is considered that the singeing of the hair closes the ends of the tubes, and thus preserves the natural juice in it, which tubes are left open and unprotected by cutting with scissors. We strongly advise you to consult your dictionary whenever you have a letter to write.

ROSEBUD Your writing is exceedingly good, and we have no fault whatever to find with it.

MAYFLOWERS You have no business with your visitor's hat and stick. If he be acquainted with the rules of polite society, of course he will bring them into the reception room with him, and put them upon the floor or upon a chair. He could not leave them in the hall unless staying in the house.

VIRGINIA White gloves must be worn at a wedding, but not so white boots.

HOME-MAID You may clean your kid boots with milk. To injure the digestion by eating many sweetmeats might be likely to affect your voice, or at least, disincline you to sing. If you wish for 'a recipe for a rough skin', use hard water and half dry the skin, and your skin will soon be quite rough. For a smooth skin, do the reverse.

HEPPIE Now that they have been obliged to dismiss the muff, the Parisian ladies have restored the *aumonière* or alms-bag pouch to favour, for the purpose of holding the handkerchief. It is made of black velvet and hangs at the side, but it may also be made of the same material as the dress. It is reported, too, that little bags, hung upon the arm, such as were worn by our grandmothers, are coming in again. They are made of satin, to match the colour of the toilette. The corners have small tassels, and there are also tassels to finish the cord with which the bag hangs to the arm, and on one side the initials or monogram of the owner are embroidered.

PERIWINKLE We know of no better cure for round shoulders than to wear a back-board and face-board daily, for an hour at a time, twice a day, while reading or learning your lessons.

WATERFALL The subject for the next competition in plain needlework will be Flannel Bed Jackets, for wear under nightdresses.

KELA You should wear a sort of white bathing costume, consisting of trousers and an overdress with a skirt reaching to the feet, fastened with a belt round the waist, and made of white flannel, or serge. The sleeves long to the wrists, but open, so as to be quickly removed, when the ceremony of the baptism is over.

KATHLEEN We do not think it would be nice and 'ladylike in a girls' school to challenge another school to a game of cricket or rounders'. We have already expressed an opinion in reference to the former game in connection with girls.

HESBA Nothing will prevent lime gathering inside a tea-kettle.

ICE You would not be eligible for any work in 'law-copying', on account of your handwriting, which is very bad; and the composition of your letter is not even grammatical. Surely you could improve both.

GRETCHEN We have seen melon pips threaded on fine wire, and bent into little baskets.

ALIGHTAH It would be very improper for any young girl to ride out alone, or with a riding master, unless accompanied by one or more companions. We do not consider it seemly for a girl to ride into the country even, accompanied only by her groom. Such rides should be restricted to the parks and public places.

PHOEBE To study for half an hour before breakfast might do you no harm. Leave a full hour between a meal, when concluded, and any hard study, otherwise the working of the brain will interfere with that of the digestive organs, and result, sooner or later, in ill-health.

DOLLY VARDEN You are quite right to hesitate over accepting even a flower from gentlemen with whom you have to do in your business; considering how familiar they frequently are, we strongly advise you to decline very politely with a slight bow, saying 'You must kindly excuse me, but I do not accept flowers from gentlemen.' Of course your conduct and manner must be 'all of a piece', and you should avoid joking and laughing with them.

SAVOURNEEN You cannot want a 'receipt for cracked lips' as you have never sent us any to be acknowledged; nor even a *recipe* for them, as they would not prove an agreeable acquisition. If you want a *cure* for them we should advise you to invest a penny in a little lip salve, to be had at all chemists' shops. Avoid altogether wetting your lips with the tongue — a common and injurious habit. Apply the lip salve whenever you take your daily walk, and on going to bed every night.

PINK HYACINTH We are in receipt of your penny stamp designed to be added to the subscription of similar sums from our subscribers for the Irish poor. But we are not prepared to enter into any such undertaking.

PORTIA Your inquiries of a personal character are unsuitable.

CORALINE It would be a great impertinence and breach of etiquette in any private gentleman or lady to call upon one of the royal princes or princesses, however near their residence might be.

A SIMPLE GIRL Your writing, spelling, and composition are alike shocking; the sooner you begin thinking of improving them the better. Nothing in the way of beauty could make up for such ignorance of common attainments.

SCRU We do not understand what you mean respecting the 'bad plan of making bodices meet at the back'. You could not leave that part of your dress open! So we suppose you refer to stays; and it is certainly well to leave these open at the back, as the least pressure of any hard substance on the spine might do harm.

NINA We do not require 'Ameature poetry' — whatever that may mean — but thank you all the same.

BUNDLE 'Mind your p's and q's' means 'mind your feet and your wigs', for the initial letters stand for the French words *pieds* and *queues*. In the time of Louis XIV, the wigs worn were immense, and might easily have fallen off when the profound bows were made — a step being first taken forward, and then a low bend of the whole body. So, to prevent such an accident as that above named, the dancing master used to warn his pupils as translated.

MAGPIE The author of the verses called *Home, Sweet Home,* commencing with 'Mid pleasures and palaces, though we may roam', was J. Howard Payne, who flourished 1792-1852. The song occurs in the opera of *Clari the Maid of Milan.*

E. THEL We do not think that taking tea three times a day would discolour the skin, but it would certainly weaken the digestion.

COLINA The practical way of learning to be useful is to begin by dusting the drawing-room and trying to make a pudding for dinner; both of these are easy to manage, and lie quite close to your hand at home.

SUSANNAH We advise you to banish from your mind all thoughts of being what you always call a 'goveness'. Your spelling, writing, grammar, and common style of expressing yourself render a girl, already nearly fifteen, quite incompetent to prepare for such a situation. We never before heard of such a person as a 'short-hand goveness'. From your desire to educate yourself, and thereby earn your living, we dare say you are a nice little girl, but if you applied as much zeal to be a good needlewoman, to make dresses, and to dress hair, you are still young enough to fit yourself for a good situation as a lady's maid. Or else you might learn to be a cook, and you could attend classes.

CASSIE KECK Always wet the head before taking a cold bath.

VIOLET We should imagine that you had bronchitis. Consult a doctor; and remember that it is not seemly to describe your ailments on a postcard.

FLY You need not try to improve so pretty a specimen of delicate and well-formed writing as yours. Some examples of good and bad hands have already been selected for illustrations to an article on 'The Art of Penmanship'. Had we seen yours sooner it should have been amongst them.

MADEMOISELLE There is no such word as 'mopishness', and there ought to be no such thing, if we understand what you mean by the expression.

OLD POINT Two young girls should not be seen riding in the park without a gentleman's companionship, or else the attendance of a groom.

EARNEST ADMIRER Perhaps a little weak gum-water might help you to keep your hair in order.

KEW GARDENS A 'nightingale' is a kind of jacket which was so called after Miss Nightingale, and was invented by her in the Crimean war, for the use of invalids in bed.

CORA Put some treacle into a basin, and lay a few strips of cardboard, to serve as ladders, for the cockroaches to gain access to it, and by this means you will catch them in the morning.

HOODIE The opal is said to represent hope; the garnet and ruby, constancy; the pearl, purity; and the diamond, innocence. The turquoise, prosperity; the emerald, success and love; the topaz, fidelity; the sardonyx, conjugal felicity; the cornelian, content; the amethyst, sincerity; the sapphire, truth. This list of emblematic meanings, attributed respectively to the stones enumerated, is borrowed from the Polish.

MARIHA S. FISHER We quite approve of your wish to act with perfect propriety, and to be 'a lady in mind', although your 'hands be rough'. Tell your mistress that you do not wish to go out at night with your young man; and that, if she would kindly allow you to take a walk occasionally in the daylight, you think it would be more respectable than after dusk. We think that you will have her full consent and approval.

AN UNSOPHISTICATED CHILD OF NATURE Kindly choose a shorter *nom de plume* when next you write. Do not be uneasy about your tortoise.

MAUD A housemaid of fifteen could not expect much in wages. She could only act as an 'under-housemaid' in the family of a gentleman, not having thoroughly learned her business nor attained her full height. Besides this, she could not be left in a responsible situation, in charge of the house were the family absent, or the cook out. £10 per annum would be all her services would be worth, if willing, active etc.

PUSSY Canaries seem to be in the ascendant just now. Make no difference in the diet. The canary is now an artificial bird, and has accommodated itself to an artificial mode of life. Only, do not give it hempseed as a rule. The seed is intoxicating, and the birds are therefore very fond of it.

GREEN PEA PODS Your little poodle, who will not eat 'bread and butter and sugar on it' ought to be made to wait till it is hungry. Oatmeal porridge and milk is better for it than so much meat. A little sour buttermilk rubbed on the face at night will remove the freckles.

PA'S DARLING Rub the eyebrows three or four times a day with a piece of raw onion; you must not redden the skin, however.

THIMBLE Have the black tarletan and yellow leno damped, which will take the stiffness out, and perhaps you can then ravel them out. If not, cut them into three-inch strips, and have the edges 'pinked' out; then gather them together closely, and having cut out the shape of an apron for your grate, proceed to trim it with the flounces. The foundation should be of black or yellow. You do not require a mantle; a round cape would be sufficient for the summer, or else a lace hood.

EUSTACIE wishes to know 'up to what age a girl may climb a tree?' If a pack of wolves were after you, we should advise you to climb a tree up to ninety or a hundred! Otherwise, why make yourself look so like one of Dr. Darwin's monkey-progenitors? Were there apples in the tree, we should excuse your so doing; but otherwise it is not so delightful to be up a tree, nor a suitable position for a girl.

SNOWDROP You had better make enquiries for yourself about a binder. We do not give space for answers to such uninteresting and unsuitable questions.

DULCINEA Keep fresh meat carefully covered from flies. Pepper your hams well, and beware of damp places.